Stone-Garland

Also by Dan Beachy-Quick

Poetry

North True South Bright

Spell

Mulberry

This Nest, Swift Passerine

Circle's Apprentice

gentlessness

Variations on Dawn and Dusk

Nonfiction

A Whaler's Dictionary

Wonderful Investigations

A Brighter Word Than Bright: Keats at Work

Of Silence and Song

Collaborations

Conversities, with Srikanth Reddy

Work from Memory, with Matthew Goulish

Stone-Garland

SIX POETS FROM THE GREEK
LYRIC TRADITION

Translated by
Dan Beachy-Quick

MILKWEED EDITIONS

Published 2020 by Milkweed Editions
Printed in the United States of America
Cover art and design by Mary Austin Speaker
Author photo by Kristy Beachy-Quick
20 21 22 23 24   5 4 3 2 1
First Edition

Milkweed Editions, an independent nonprofit publisher, gratefully acknowledges sustaining support from the Alan B. Slifka Foundation and its president, Riva Ariella Ritvo-Slifka; the Ballard Spahr Foundation; *Copper Nickel*; the McKnight Foundation; the National Endowment for the Arts; the National Poetry Series; the Target Foundation; and other generous contributions from foundations, corporations, and individuals. Also, this activity is made possible by the voters of Minnesota through a Minnesota State Arts Board Operating Support grant, thanks to a legislative appropriation from the arts and cultural heritage fund. For a full listing of Milkweed Editions supporters, please visit milkweed.org.

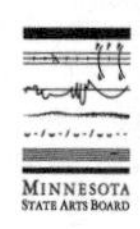

McKNIGHT FOUNDATION

Names: Beachy-Quick, Dan, 1973- translator.
Title: Stone-garland : six poets from the Greek lyric tradition / translated by Dan Beachy-Quick.
Description: Minneapolis, Minnesota : Milkweed Editions, 2020. | Series: Seedbank | Summary: "Translations of poems and poem fragments from the Greek lyric tradition"-- Provided by publisher.
Identifiers: LCCN 2020010537 (print) | LCCN 2020010538 (ebook) | ISBN 9781571315328 (paperback) | ISBN 9781571317285 (ebook)
Subjects: LCSH: Greek poetry--Translations into English.
Classification: LCC PA3622 B43 2020 (print) | LCC PA3622 (ebook) | DDC 884.008--dc23
LC record available at https://lccn.loc.gov/2020010537
LC ebook record available at https://lccn.loc.gov/2020010538

Milkweed Editions is committed to ecological stewardship. We strive to align our book production practices with this principle, and to reduce the impact of our operations in the environment. We are a member of the Green Press Initiative, a nonprofit coalition of publishers, manufacturers, and authors working to protect the world's endangered forests and conserve natural resources. Stone-Garland was printed on acid-free 100% postconsumer-waste paper by Sheridan Books Inc.

Contents

Introduction

Of the first poets, we hear rumors, but have no poems.

I heard Orpheus took his lyre and walked down into death. For centuries some philosophers have mocked the poet, lacking the courage to die himself, and going alive into the underworld to return his Eurydice to light. But others have worshipped him as one might worship a god; he might well be defined in the classical sense as semi-divine. He sang to the striking of his lyre songs of the world, and what he sang came to him: fish leapt up from the steel-blue sea, the blue-backed swallows flocked about him in such numbers it seemed his song sang out the center of a storm cloud. Rocks gathered at his feet when he sang stone; when he sang trees the birches stepped to the tune. On his wedding day his bride, bitten by a snake, was stolen by death into death. In memory so deep it precedes the mind, Socrates gives an etymology of the word "hero." He claims that ‘ἡρως and ’ἑρος—*hero* and *love*—bloom from the same root; a homonym, ’ἑρρω, means *to go limping*, means *to disappear into one's own harm*. So we know Orpheus limped into hell, singing as he disappeared. On his journey down, the cursed ones who live there listened: Tantalus listened to the poet, drank a handful of water, ate a grape, for the music made the water and the vine stand still; Sisyphus leaned his back against the boulder that no longer rolled down the hill. Song's eternity is a different eternity than the punishment that reigns in Hades—an eternity that liberates those condemned to timelessness. Just as Eurydice was learning the names of the flowers in hell and committing the strange sounds to memory, her husband arrived. Hades agreed to let her leave death if Orpheus sang the whole way up to earth's surface and never turned around to see if she followed.

So Orpheus walked back singing and limped his way up again. The poet H.D. imagines he turns around just as Eurydice can see the sunlight on the singer's cheek, just as the air begins to smell of violets. I like to think of it the same. Orpheus turned around to see if Eurydice followed, and so she tumbled back into darkness, into death, never to emerge again. A scholiast might suggest some lessons for the would-be translator—that the poem bears a strange relation to life and death, that one might need to learn to trust that the song's deepest care occurs not in the poem but follows after it, that one must look back even as one knows one should not, and what we love the most keeps itself at the greatest distance from us, and perhaps it can be no other way.

I heard that Linus, Orpheus's brother, first to sing laments, was killed by his father, Apollo, who emptied his quiver into the boy for rivaling him in a singing contest. The word for such a contest in Greek is an "agony." Rainer Maria Rilke says that he can hear Linus still, "vibrations in the void." I heard another rumor that Linus, teacher of song, was killed by his student Heracles, the hero angry at being reprimanded for playing the harp so poorly. A scholiast might teach us of fathers that our sources are threats; a scholiast might teach us a student is dangerous, too. The translator might feel both threat and threatened at once.

I heard Arion sailed away from home to sing at royal courts and, when he made his fortune, hired a boat to carry him back. The merchant-sailors, once on sea, decided to kill the poet and steal his wealth. They gave Arion a choice about how he wanted to die: by blade or by jumping in the ocean. He chose the ocean. He changed into his many-colored silk robes and with lyre in hand sang a last song on the prow of the ship and then jumped in. The boat sailed on and so the men aboard did not see that a dolphin came and sped the poet to his homeland. There he told the archon what happened. Arion hid when the ship came to port. Asked where the poet was they told the archon that he died in a foreign land. Then Arion stepped out from hiding; his murderers were caught, condemned, and killed in turn. What the scholiast might say about Arion's story I cannot quite guess. Maybe it is you sing and step into the water; maybe it is you sing and step into the world, and some kind of justice follows.

*

A poem neither ancient nor Greek has come to speak most clearly to me of what I hope might be found in these pages. The poem is George Oppen's "Psalm," whose devotion to sincere forms of clarity brings to our eyes the clear air lit up by the old Greek sun:

Veritas sequitur . . .

In the small beauty of the forest
The wild deer bedding down—
That they are there!

Their eyes
Effortless, the soft lips
Nuzzle and the alien small teeth
Tear at the grass

The roots of it
Dangle from their mouths

Scattering earth in the strange woods.
They who are there.

Their paths
Nibbled thru the fields, the leaves that shade them
Hang in the distances
Of sun

The small nouns
Crying faith
In this in which the wild deer
Startle, and stare out.

The poem turns toward the existence of all that is not us, and in doing so, we might find ourselves in the world's grasp—the deer that make their home in the wild world—and we have to learn again how the world grows wild. They eat the very plants in which they make their bed, and against the cosmic glare of the sun's rational light, the leaves of the tree offer shade, offer refuge. The roots root down in the irrational, in the lyric radicals, and it is these roots that dangle from the mouths of the deer "scattering earth in the strange woods." Time works its lesser destruction in the forest and in the field, in the archive and on the poem, but the vital need to live that tears the roots up from the ground only to scatter the seed back into the strange woods works a truer violence. The lodgepole pine releases its seed in fire; there are seeds that only gain vitality passing through the digestive tract of the animal that eats them; some ideas bloom only by virtue of the poem being written, and if to read is as digestive a process as it is an intellectual one (and I think it is), then we find ourselves, just like the deer, with the dirt falling out our mouths as we consider the roots.

Maybe we come then to a genuine poetic faith—one in which the words themselves speak our faith for us. We come to know our devotion by learning to listen to the words we speak. It is not enough to learn the words; one must learn to learn from them. The "small nouns" cry out to the deer and the deer stare back; but the stone is just as startled; and so is the tree; and when in the strange woods we learn to see ourselves by those eyes that in their startle stare back at us, we've come to the edge of the wilderness in which the poem offers us its greatest gift: we know ourselves from outside ourselves, and the work of the mind that seems so inwardly riddled inverts and, as poets have long known, "I is other."

One of the words for "reading" in ancient Greek is αναγ-ιγν'ώσκω. It means *to know again*. But that "knowing" is a curious one, related to the word γίγνομαι, whose definition, in its beautiful complexity, offers a sense—the taste of the *humus* on the tongue—of what poetic knowledge might be: *to come into being, to be born, to be produced, to fall due (as a debt), to come to pass (as an event)*. The poem offers to us a strange opportunity which is also a strange responsibility. To read calls back into being the long cares the poem embraces. It is not enough simply to read an ancient poem and have some fleeting glimpse that the emotions, thoughts, and experiences may be related to our own lives. Better is to sense that poetry (the reading, writing, and translating of it), is—like Socrates's sense of philosophy—a maieutic art, though in a poem it is something other than an idea that is midwifed into existence. What it is, I don't exactly know. The deer and the strange woods, yes, but also something more—something Emerson sensed when he wrote that "every word was once a poem." A conscious seed which, as the oak-seed has within it the possibility of every angled branch and drooping leaf, might have within it the wilderness entire—where the deer bed down, where they nibble their paths through the forest—of what world it is our minds come to be. A poem properly read asks us to give birth to ourselves, and knowing is a different process than we could guess—it happens outside of us, and the mind is the thing that occurs in the words when they are spoken or sung; the mind begins in the poem sown in the blank page.

*

It makes me happy how error so often leads the way and makes intent a fool's errand. A rhyme can trick the mind into spurious relations all the more true for being unprovable. A shared sound can open a threshold in the bramble, and if one can't crawl through the gap into the old meadow, one can glimpse the verdant ancient field and take a breath.

The word for song in ancient Greek is 'αοιδή. As cloud drifts into cloud on a summer's day and drifts back out again, words of similar sonic shape drift into song. There is the cloud called *eternity*, 'αίδιος; there is the cloud called *shame*, 'αἶδώς; and there is the cloud called the *idea-of-all-that's-seen*, εἶδος. As inaccurate as it may be to compare the translator to the child leaning back in long grass and watching the clouds play at similes, something in the vision rings true. Could it be true that in the deepest phenomenal level of what it is a poem is, that song is both a form of shame and a form of eternity, that the poem seeks an immortality that would forsake the very idea of the world that—in its beauty that uses the eye to break apart the mind—the poem cherishes daily and truly? I feel it in the poems that fill this book. The logic of how life should be lived decays so wondrously into the more difficult possibilities of what life is. Ideal beauty has as the opposite side of its potent fact the desire beauty creates—and desire walks toward eternity with a limp and a blushing cheek, singing all the way, followed by all who listen, who learn to want by the wanting of the song itself, which, as long as the singing doesn't cease, as long as it doesn't turn around, will not lose us to the fathomless eons of time.

It is a deeply human realization our presence in these poems might give us.

A reminder that I am human, and so are you.

The scholiast's final lesson.

I have a mouth so that I can sing another's song.

Note on Translation

Your hands should smell of the flowers you're gathering when you read an *anthology*. The collection of poems is a kind of bouquet loosely bound, a flower-logic, a petal-theory, a blossom-word. It's in honor of that lovely word that I've gathered these poems together, selecting from poets I admire the poems I most love. I've imagined this anthology in light of the *Palatine Anthology*, and the sepulchral epigrams that can be found there, wherein one poet writes an imagined epitaph for another. It is the kind of consideration that lets the gravestone speak for the poet who otherwise is now silent. At the ruins of Delphi the stray cats wander among the poppies and marble slabs. That vision hovers in my mind, that memory.

I imagine this book as a country graveyard overgrown by wildflowers and long grasses no mower could think to cull back. The blades of grass would dull the scythe. The graveyard is filled with broken stones, some legible and some not, some whole and others but a fragment with a few words etched on it. Some of these may seem to belong together—barest insinuation of care that crosses the gaps between the stones. And at the end of each wandering reading, a gravestone complete, written by another poet about the poet whose broken words have lent your mind an odor that might best be called *thought*. As such, you'll find poems here constructed from disparate fragments, held together not by fact, but by resonance. Others are offered whole. I've tried to offer some sense of the wondrous and strange complexity of certain Greek words. The definition for λόγος meanders from *computation* to *account of (money)* to *measure* to *plea (in a court of law)* to *ratio* to *theoretical or hypothetical speech* to *logic* long before it ever gets to the surface we're most familiar with, *a word.* The word φρήν means, simultaneously, *midriff, heart (as seat of passions), mind,* and *will.* I've come to think any word given back to its lyric nature carries within it similar perplexities, and to what degree I could allow the poems to be a version of a heart that thinks, or a mind that pulses, I did so. Preferring to let the poems capture what they could of the personality of the poet singing them, I privileged the spoken over the metrical, trusting that a vision of the world the poet allows us to glimpse will adjust the ear accordingly.

I hope the book might be a way to spend a pleasant hour or two, a walled cemetery of a kind, where cost of admission is to leave hectic cares at the gate, and all that's left is that morning light, a light in which no hours pass, a light not made of time, in which one comes—if not face-to-face with these poets of the past, which might be impossible—to stand by their burial mounds and feel the thrum of the lyre plucked underground.

Simonides

A poet praised for the pity his poems put in the heart of those who heard them, Simonides was also revered for his honesty and wisdom. Anecdotes abound. He spent the end of his long life in Sicily, friend of the tyrant Hiero of Syracuse, who asked the poet "what god is or what he is like." Getting no immediate answer, the tyrant asked again the next day, and the next until, exasperated with the poet, he asked why no response came. "Because the longer I think about it, the fainter become my hopes of an answer," Simonides said. Other silences bear themselves out in the poet's life. He considered paintings poems that stay quiet, and poems paintings that speak. He noted a wisdom passed down through ages, that "he had often felt sorry after speaking but never after keeping quiet." The deeply human humility inside such notice unfolds in other realms. Thero (another tyrant of Sicily), angered at Hiero, went with his army to the river Gela to make war, but Simonides showed up before the battle and ended the conflict before it began—in the scholiast's fragment where the tale is recorded, it's suggested the poet brought his lyre. To Hiero and the Spartan king Pausanias he gave the same advice: to remember they were human.

Being human is a complex situation, even for the wise, even for the humble. Although Simonides was cherished for his fine qualities, other aspects of his character have been mocked for centuries. Simonides is known as the first poet to accept payment for his poems, and so found himself often in the company (employment) of tyrants, wealthy merchants, ancestral aristocrats. He lived a long life, perhaps into his early nineties, which instilled in him a worldliness that runs counter to romantic ideals of who and what a poet should be. Hiero's wife, asking Simonides if it's better to be wealthy or wise, is told "Wealthy; for I see the wise spending their days at the doors of the wealthy." All things grow old, he claimed, except moneymaking; and kind deeds grow old most quickly. Xenophanes called him a skinflint. A tale "well-known" has Simonides sitting between two boxes, one empty and the other full—the latter filled with money, the former filled with favors. Simonides even sold most of the gifts Hiero gave him for cash, keeping scant items for himself, "so that all may see Hiero's magnificence," he said, "and my moderation."

The poet seeking payment finds himself under cruel roofs. Scopas, a nobleman from Thessaly, hired Simonides to write a victory ode. Scopas held a lavish feast and ordered Simonides to read his ode out loud. The poem extolled the heroes Castor and Pollux, whose praise took more lines than the praise of Scopas, whose victory the heroes were meant to garland. Before all at the banquet Scopas refused to pay in full the promised fee, saying he would purchase only those lines that mention him, and the gods could pay their own debts. Cast to the side of the festivities, last to take food from the bowls passed around, Simonides was told by a servant that two young men waited for him in the street. Simonides stood up and walked out the large room, wandered through the house to the door, but when he opened it, no one was there. Just then, as he looked at that emptiness that called him out from the party, the roof of the house collapsed and killed everyone at the feast. The bodies were crushed beyond recognition and could only be returned to their mourning families by the help of Simonides, who remembered where each person was sitting. For the poet who said "the word is the image of the thing," it must have been simple to see, as if hovering above the rubble, the names of those underneath it. So the poet founded a system of memory, associating word to place, and he's credited with creating the art of mnemonics.

Though sources disagree, Simonides was born around 540 BCE and died during the 78th Olympiad (468–464 BCE). His life spanned the glory of Athens, where he first lived in the court of the tyrant Hipparchus, and to which he returned during the Persian Wars. He was born in Ceos, but we know little of his death, save what the poet Callimachus mentions in a sepulchral epigram. The people of Acragas, a town on Sicily's southern coast, built a large burial mound outside the city, stone piled on stone. Phoenix, a general of the city, took apart the mound and used the stones to build a tower. It is a sad but fitting last image, testament to the poet who offered such humane advice to the mighty, praising simple goodness even as he recognized wealth's force, that his humble final home, dedicated to Zeus, guardian of strangers who wander the earth (and who isn't in the end just such a stranger), should be pulled apart and turned into the pillar of another man's pride. The powerful are deaf to the poems they commission; the vicious live inside the deaths they do not honor.

FRAGMENT ON ORPHEUS

. . . and countless
birds above your head flew about,
the fish leapt straight up
out the steel dark blue waters
at your beautiful song . . .

MOTHER AND CHILD, CAST OUT TO SEA

—for Cedar, Mark, and Silver

When in the coffin
intricately carved
the wind made the wood tremble
and the horrid sea crashed
down, with wet cheeks wetter yet,
around Perseus she threw her loving arms
and said, "Child, what suffering I hold."

But you sleep, your
suckling heart slumbers
on somber planks bronze-bolted
in this no-star-shining night, you
drop down in the deep mourning-veil dark,
of the sea-spray's thick mist above
your hair as by a wave covered
you are careless, careless of the wind's
keen howl, lying
within my purple shawl, your lovely face.
If this terror was terror for you
you'd turn your small ears
to my hushed words.

I tell you, sleep as still in my womb, baby;
go to sleep, sea; go to sleep, my depthless trouble.

Out from your mind let some change appear,
Father Zeus.
For what in my prayer is too bold or not just,

look aside,
forgive me.

OF A CASTRATED WORSHIPPER OF CYBELE

When Gallas fled the winter storm's falling snow
    and came under a gift-of-the-god slab of rock,
he'd just wiped from his hair the drench, when—
    following the straight path of his footprints—
an ox-eating lion came to the hollow.
    But he struck hard with the flat of his hand
the holy drum, and all the cave cried out the sharp sound.
    The wood-dwelling wild beast could not bear
Cybele's wonder-loud fury, rushed to the wood's edge
    afraid of the half-woman, servant to the goddess,
who hung up—to honor Rhea—this garment
    and hung up her braid of golden hair.

FRAGMENT

Difficult to build by hand a man
truly good and well-built and with a mind,
    foursquare and made without a flaw . . .

        —seven lines missing—

And the tuneful words Pittacus dealt out
are nothing for me, though strung together
    by a wise man: "It's difficult to cleave to goodness,"
he said. Only a god has this gift. A man can't
    not abide with evil
when ill luck leaves him lacking what's pure.
Good luck lets any man be good,
    But if luck is bad, the man is bad.
Mostly, it's best for him whom the gods keep
    inside their love.

And so I don't waste my strength
to seek in hollow things meaning, I don't
    throw my life away on impossible hopes—.
And of the all-blameless man who plucks his fruit
from the orchards of the earth?
If among our wide numbers is such a one, I'll come tell you.
I applaud and love any man
who knowingly shuts himself away
and does nothing shameful. Not even the gods
fight against necessity.

—two lines missing—

...I am not one who loves to give blame: for me
a man who isn't bad suffices, who doesn't act as if he has
no hands, who understands what for the city is just.
The man mind-sound, body-sound: I don't
cast fault his way. All things are
beautiful, noble, fair—
in which no shameful thing is mixed.
But men are infinite
    generations of fools.

What man who trusts his mind would praise Cleoboulos,
dweller in Lindos, who placed against
streams ever-flowing, flowers and springtime,
sun's all-flame and golden moon
and the seawater's whorls, the might of his gravestone?
All things are less than the gods. Mortal men
can in the palms of their hands break into pieces
precious stone. His choice
pleased him, the fool.

You are a man, so don't say what tomorrow will be.
Never, seeing a man happy in the world, think to know
what time will be: not even a damselfly's
random flight moves so swift.

We came to wear death's yoke under a hill in Dirphys, our grave
paid for by the people, the river Euripus nearby pouring out;
it's not not-just, destroyed in our lovely youth,
waiting the attack of that rough cloud of war.

*

Glory's quenchless flame these men placed on their loved country,
then threw around themselves death's dark-as-a-swallow's-
back cloud.
None are dead though they have died: down from above, their virtue
is honored, and leads them up from the house of Hades.

*

Once in the breasts of these men Ares bathed
in blood-bright drops arrows long-barbed:
in place of dead men spear-struck, memory-mounds—
of lifeless, having-life men—covered in fearless dust.

*

Lean, my long ash-spear, against this tall pillar,
and stay there, holy to all-word-uttering Zeus.
Your bronze-tip like an old man is worn out
from much, in dreadful battle, furious shaking.

*

Stranger, go tell the Spartans that these men
    lie here, listening for their words.

*

Death finds even the battle-fleer.

All things come to one single horrible Charybdis—
all things great and virtuous, all wealth.

FRAGMENT

of sky   of sea
  some black-turning-black force
    void desolate of mortals and also
  the goat-shanked gods divine

SEPULCHRAL EPIGRAM FOR SIMONIDES, BY CALLIMACHUS

Not even Camarina would be so truly bad
  as removing, rock by overhanging rock,
a sacred man's tomb. Once it was my grave:
  above me the men of Acragas heaped
stones, standing in awe of Zeus, guest-protector.
  An evil man tore it down to ruins—
anyone, maybe even you, have heard of him—
  Phoenix, the city's heartless leader.
He built my tomb into a tower, shameless
  before the etched words that speak me,
a son of Leoprepeos, laid to rest there,
  a holy-man from Ceos, who filled with wonders
himself, first made known memory's work;
  nor did I tremble before you, Polydeuces,
didn't fear you and your brother, when
  alone among the invited guests
you brought me outside, *ai ai*, the house
  when the roof-beams crashed down,
and Crannon's house fell on mighty Scopas.

Anacreon / Anacreonata

Before the altar of Hera in Samos, as reported by Apuleius in his *Flowers of Rhetoric*, is a statue of the boy Anacreon loved, and whose name, Bathyllus—like a broken column's stones among the green grass and red poppies of the ruin—is littered throughout the fragments remaining. The statue is singing a song to the tyrant Polycrates, who also loved the boy, and the song is a poem of Anacreon's, sung "for friendship's sake." Apt enough, that the boy would sing the song of one who loved him to another man who did the same, and for the brief flicker of time a lyric poem lives on the lips (moment that pauses time and makes it almost eternal); the song itself kept love open—disarmed rivalry, pettiness, jealousy; confirmed that love is larger than the bounds of the body in which desire is felt, kept, and satisfied. That the statue no longer exists might also be one of love's lessons—the rumor alone, ancient as it is, lets us see the boy singing if not wholly hear the song.

Spurning epic seriousness, Anacreon sang of his life's devotions, and his "life was devoted to the love of boys and women and to song." Many ancient accounts add wine to the list of the poet's erotic faiths, and Anacreon lived a life long enough to indulge himself more often than most. Born in Teos, he lived for eighty-five years, ending the wide span of his life in Athens. There, it is said, he saw the tragedies of Aeschylus performed—those plays that the tragedian described as mere "slices from Homer's banquet," so different from the poet's lyrics of infatuation and drunken love. That fragment of text places his life loosely in the sixth century BCE (570–485), alive during the reign of Cyrus the Great, friend with the poet Simonides who, according to Plato, was highly paid by the tyrant Hipparchus to never leave Anacreon's side. Well-known for the delight his poetry gave—delight that sings of delights—the poet also served as moral warning for those unable to praise the luxury that birthed the beauty of his poems. "Asked why he did not write hymns to gods but to boys, he replied, 'Because they are my gods.'" Love blasphemes to stay true to love.

Living such love leads to other depictions: a man with lust in his eye, robes trailing on the ground, limping with one foot bare and playing the lyre, singing a song to Bathyllus who, I'm guessing, is nowhere to be found. Nowhere save in the name embedded in song. Anacreon's death arrives as one of those fated ironies that overwhelms fact by letting us see the poet's face. This ever-drunk, ever-desiring poet dies when a single raisin gets stuck in his throat. Let the tale be a lesson that every grape should be translated into wine; and let us see in the doomed sanctuary of our own minds the statue Pausanius saw in his travels through Greece, standing in the Athenian acropolis between figures of Pericles and Sappho, dear Anacreon, caught in stone "singing when he is drunk."

*

In the tenth-century manuscript that contained the many volumes of the *Palatine Anthology* one also finds two volumes containing the poems known as the *Anacreonata*—poems written centuries after Anacreon's life but written under his name. In the first poem, Anacreon himself, old but handsome still, still amorous, walks up to the nameless speaker, takes the garland from his own head and gives it to the other man, and the crown smelled of Anacreon. "Fool that I was, I held it up and fastened it on my brow—and to this very day I have not ceased to be in love." It is not known if it is one poet or many that wrote in the voice of Anacreon, singing the ancient loves, drunk on old wine ever new, singing the old names new . . . Bathyllus . . . The poems—complete, free of time's fragmentation that leaves us Anacreon's poems in tatters and ruins scattered through other texts—were written as late as Roman times. The facts get lost left to their own devices; the face gathers itself around the voice, and though nothing is known, the heart quickens with impossible presence. I can have faith in such a poetry: to be in love with another's love, and to write the songs that keep that love alive.

[*Note*: To honor that poetic transformation of anonymous life back into Anacreon's, I've woven together Anacreon's fragments with poems selected from the *Anacreonata*, so that both voices can be read together as if they were one: a garland twines together more than a single strand.]

FIELD-SONG

We call you blessed, cicada,
when from the high bent-branch arch of trees
you have drunk your pure little dew,
how like a king, like an arrow-string, you sing.
You are one who is all things,
in the far fields you are as all you see,
great as the woods that bear the nut-bearing trees.
You are dear friend of ground-tilling men,
never hindering, never damaging, the crop;
those who cannot not die hold you in honor
as summer's sweet prophet;
the Muses love you, kiss you;
the Sun himself loves you, kisses you,
and gave you the clear-voiced plow-path of your song.
Old age does not wear you away,
wise one, earth-born, song-lover—
with no suffering, without spilling blood,
you are so near, so like, the gods.

No one, or none, or no . . .
but yours is a timid heart,
bright-faced girl; your mother,
cherishing you, thinks her care
keeps you close in the house . . .
But you fled to the hyacinth fields
where out from the leather strap
Love halts her horses:
. . . into their midst you ran eager
. . . among the many you darted quick
and their scared hearts fluttered—
o Herotima, on the road, the public road

You, Thracian foal, why do you
    look at me with eyes turning aside,
you pitiless flee, you
    imagine me wise in nothing;
but I know you—and could
    put in your mouth the bit
beautifully; I could, reins in hand,
    turn you about the turning-stone
in the drama-race; now, you eat
    grass in meadows and lightly
leap, you play as a child plays,
    because you have no horse-skilled
one to guide or mount you.

LOVE'S CHORE

Lovely pigeon wild,
from where, from where did you fly?
From where? With pine-perfumes of balsam-air
your panting breath drops down its odor;
you come down in a mist, like little rain.
Who are you? And who cares for you?

"Anacreon sent me
to a child, to Bathyllus,
that boy so suddenly conqueror
and tyrant of us all.
Love herself took me in her hand
and sold me for my little song;
for Anacreon, many times,
I carry messages.
And now what letters from this man
I carry safe away!
And he tells me with open face
that he will set me free—
but even if he releases me,
I will remain for him his slave.
Why should I need to fly
from mountains down to fields
and make my seat in the trees
to eat—what?—some coarse, wild thing?
Now I eat cake
snatched from the hands
of Anacreon himself,

and to drink he gives me
the wine he drinks himself, his oath to love.
Our drinking done, I begin my dance,
my despot striking the tune,
I cast a shadow on his face with my wings;
and when his tongue lulls itself to sleep,
I lie down on the strings of the lyre.
There, you know it all—. Now go away—.
You gave me to endless chattering,
man, like I'm some carrion-crow."

What Love in roses
didn't see, wounded him:
the bee hushed asleep—
struck on the finger,
his loud voice cried out.
He ran like a gnat-catcher
darts after gnats, aimless
as gnats fly he also ran
to beautiful Cytherea.
"*Olowla*, mother," he cried,
"I have died, and I am dying,
a useless death—
that small, winged snake
the farmers call a honeybee
stung me. *Olowla,*" he cried.
She replied, "If the sting
of the bees works such
suffering, how much do you
think they suffer, Love,
those ones in pain, you strike?"

For my words children might cherish me:
graceful songs I sing, graceful words
I know how to speak.

POETIC ECONOMY

—for Cassandra Cleghorn and Jeffrey Levine

When the runaway slave to whom I'm slave, the gold
dust that drops through fingers, flees from me
on rapid, made-swift-by-wind feet
(always, always fleeing from me)
I do not chase him: who
wants to hunt what he hates?
I fall suddenly back, I drift away,
fugitive from that fugitive gold—
my mind is my heart is my lungs
and I give my pains to a morning breeze to bear away
as a mother bears a child, and taking my lyre
I sing the songs that sing love.
But when my heart teaches me to despise him,
the fugitive suddenly speaks,
bringing me strong drink and drunken plans,
that careless I take him
and neglect my lyre, so pleasing to the ear.
Faithless, faithless gold,
fruitlessly you spell-bind me with magic-tricks—
more than gold, the gut-strings
of the lyre hide sweet desires.
Tricks, yes, ill-will, jealousy, burnings-of-the-heart,
you give such love to men—
but the lyre brings to bridal chambers painless
goblets, big-bellied, mixing longing with long care
and love. You flee when you want to flee;
but I would not leave at home my lyre's song.

You please faithless, deceitful strangers
instead of the Muses.
But for me, striker-of-the-lyre-strings, near my heart
the Muse dwells, neighbor to my mind,
she makes her home.
Go ahead, you—ring out your agitated plea!
Shine up like a shield shines your dizzy puzzle of light!

My temples already gray
and my head white,
youth's grace no longer
near, my teeth are old,
no longer life's sweet
muchness, it has gone
missing: time. I groan
often in dread of Tartarus,
for that most hidden room
in Hades is most terrible.
Grievous is the under-path—
before you it opens,
and he who steps down
never again walks up.

FRAGMENTS; OR, BROKEN STONES

. . . and you will
make the neighbors speak me ill . . .

. . . mischief wages war on the doorkeeper . . .

. . . you cut off the blameless flower of your soft hair . . .

. . . Love's burden . . .

. . . an urn holding in its hollow celery-stalks . . .

. . . I took myself inside the earth . . .

. . . and carried the great laws out . . .

SEPULCHRAL EPIGRAM FOR ANACREON, BY SIMONIDES

Vine, all-god-soothing, nurse of drunkards, grape-mother of harvests,
who grows, in tangled braids of tendrils twined, like a wreath—
twist your way to the top of the pillar of Anacreon's grave
and plant your root in the fine dirt of this burial mound;
that he, lover of heavy wine and, yes, the torch-bearing, crowned lover
of revels; yes, this lover of boys, striking night-long the lyre's
curved shell,
though fallen under the ground, may above his head have the bright
spray of twigs that bear in due season the grapes' shine,
and always may the soft storm's pure water rain on him, so the
ancient man
may breathe again the gentle grass's green scent his lips once
breathed out.

Archilochus

Myth and man—as for Homer himself—are inseparable in Archilochus, alive five hundred years after the Trojan War. Here's the tale of how he became a poet:

When Archilochus was still a young man, his father Telesicles asked him to take a cow to town and sell it. Archilochus rose early, moon making dim the stars near it in the still dark sky, and on the way to town saw a group of nine women. He approached them to talk, and they joked and flirted with him. I like to think the air smells green as the eastern horizon turns the slightest shade of pink. The women asked him if he was taking the cow to town to sell it, and he said that he was. They offered to buy the cow at a fair price, and when Archilochus agreed, the cow and the women vanished. He found a lyre at his feet. He took the lyre home, astounded. He told his father what happened, and his father walked the path to town, searching everywhere for the cow. Not finding it, he went to the oracle at Delphi, and the god spoke: "Immortal and renowned in song among men, Telesicles, will be whichever son of yours first speaks to you as you leap from your ship onto your beloved homeland." Archilochus was the first of his sons to greet him.

Archilochus wrote in the *iambic* tradition, a meter familiar to modern readers, but anciently a poetry of sharp bite and cruel blame. Some speculate the meter held religious significance, connected to the secret rites of Demeter and Dionysus, and ancient commentators claim of Archilochus's lineage devotion to these gods. The tale told of his engagement to one of the daughters of Lycambes, Neoboule, is infamous in the ancient world, and painful to contemporary ears. The future father-in-law broke the promise of the marriage, and in response or in revenge, Archilochus wrote a long poem decrying Lycambes as a breaker of oaths and his daughters as sexually impure. In shame, the daughters hanged themselves; according to some stories, their father committed suicide as well.

Such spite cast a wary fame around Archilochus, and poems abound in the *Palatine Anthology* warning the traveler who unwittingly steps on the poet's tomb that furious wasps will attack him. But the ancient mind considers depths that trouble the surface of our judgment. Some commentators see Archilochus in his anger as upholder of holy laws—not to break oaths, not to break the mores of sexual fidelity. "How much better it is," says Dio Chrysostom, "to revile and to reveal each person's stupidity and baseness than to court favor through one's words and corrupt listeners with praise." But other commentators see "a man who displayed his poetic skill in a subject matter that is extremely base and lewd and who revealed a character that is licentious and impure." Archilochus reveals himself in his poems as an adulterer and coward, lustful and arrogant, shameless where he should feel shame. He suffers himself the faults for which he darts his blame at the hearts of others, and whether this makes him hypocrite absolute or a figure of strange and unexpected sympathy, I cannot say myself. Because he abandoned his shield in battle and ran away, and for his attack on the family of Lycambes, Sparta destroyed all his work extant in the city, fearing his verses would defile the youth who read them. At the same time, for centuries Archilochus was considered a poet second in stature only to Homer himself, a man beloved of the Muses who bestowed upon him his lyre, and who Apollo proclaimed "to be a man of piety."

Apollo's opinion carried past the poet's death—but gods and poets both stake claims in immortality. Archilochus was killed in battle by a man named Calondas, nicknamed Corax. When Corax came to ask favors of the Pythian god, the oracle refused his admittance, claiming he polluted the ground he stood on for killing a man sacred to the Muses. Corax, forced to flee the temple, sought some way to appease Archilochus's soul in heaven and so free himself from the anger of the god. His voice could not be heard in holy realms because he killed a poet endowed with voice by the gods. No doubt, though it is nowhere recorded, the poor wanderer was stung many times by many wasps in his travels, and dropped many tears on many stones, said his prayers, hoped to atone.

TWO VARIATIONS ON THE SAME THEME

I am servant to the drawn-back-arrow-string God of War
    and know the lovely gifts of the Muses

*

. . . both servant to the god War-like
    and of the lovely Muses am gift-strong

TWO FRAGMENTS

Many tricks the fox knows,
    the hedgehog one,
        but that one is great.

*

        . . . and I know one great thing:
    to answer hurt done me
with fearsome harm.

ON THE WISDOM OF COWARDICE

Some jerk of Saia gloats over my shield,
    blameless tool I abandoned in a bush—
I wasn't wanting to—. I saved myself.
    What do I care about that shield?
Fuck it. Some other time, I'll find one just as good.

A NECKLACE OF LEWD CHARMS

. . . in deep shadow they leaned back against the wall. . .

*

. . . damp crotch . . .

*

                . . . cock swollen
        as a Prienian ass,
stud stuffed full with grain devoured . . .

*

        . . . like a Thracian man or Phrygian sucking beer
through a straw, she bent her head down, working hard . . .

*

                                    . . . the kingfisher
on the promontory stone flapped its joyous wings . . .

*

. . . out the pipe into the honey-jar . . .

*

. . . and there was much foam about her mouth . . .

*

. . . if only I could bring myself to touch Neoboule's hand just so . . .

A POEM TORN IN HALF

the surrounding smoke they made[
in warships, spear-shafts d[
men are tearing, and he wilts[
in the sunlight, courage and[
great longing for[
of Naxians able to f[
of trees cut sharp down[
men hold back[
this would for all soldiers m[
as in the past without anger[
and of brothers[
of whom they cut off[
beat down beneath plague-like blows[
these things in my soul, my thinking heart[
abysmal deep[
but all the same dead[
knows now, if you[
of words who is destined[
some men in Thasos[
and Torone[
some men in swift ships[
and from Paros t[
and of the same mother born[
soul, heart, but[
fire now all around[
in the suburbs k[
they ever-scorch the earth[

violent men overrun[
readying for the road[
nothing lucky, nothing on the right[

TWO FRAGMENTS

She delighted in holding the myrtle's tender branch—
also the rose, lovely flower.

*

. . . on shoulder
and back her hair's falling shadow . . .

LOVE POEM

"... holding off wholly
is nervous courage,
but if your heart goads you straight on
there is in this house
one now longing much,
a virgin lovely, delicate. I think
her body blameless
in the eye, made for your love."
So she spoke. And I spoke my part:
"Daughter of Amphimedo,
a woman good and faithful,
who now the earth holds in deep decay,
the goddess offers
young men many delights
beyond that treasure spot divine. Any
one of them will do, but
time quietly darkens these things.
You and I together will consider the holy
matters. Ask me anything,
I'll obey. Many things, I'll—.
Beneath the wall's high stones, by the gate,
love, hold no grudge.
Know this now: I'll hold
in my hands the scent of the herb-thick garden.
Let some other man
have Neoboule. Phew—

she's overripe, soft to the touch, twice your age,
bloom fallen off the girl
and what grace she had before
not on her. Nothing satisfies the woman's frenzied,
past all measure, lust.
Give her to the crow-dark depths
from where no one returns. Having such a wife,
I'd be the source of joy
for my neighbor's cruel laughter.
You I want much more: you not faithless, you
not two-faced. She was sharp,
clever, made many her lovers.
But I'm worried I press on in haste—
giving birth, like her,
to creatures blind, untimely."
So I spoke. Taking the girl, I laid her down
in a blooming cloud of flowers
and leaned back.
I covered her with a soft cloak, and cradling
her neck in my bent arm,
like a fawn, she grew still.
Holding her and gently with my hands I cupped
her young breasts,
pinched the stiff pink tips,
every part of her beautiful body I touched,
and shot off my hot, bright force,
grasping loosely her golden hair.

TWO FRAGMENTS

So human hearts, Glaucus son of Leptines, come to be for
mortals—
as Zeus brings day after changing day, hearts also change . . .

*

. . . and hearts think the same as the world they encounter . . .

LOVE POEM

Your skin no longer blooms tender, dry already
your furrow dead to sweet longing of plows,
age pulls down your face away from desire—
it's true: many breaths have planted winter winds
in the earth of you, too many many times . . .

-x shield
-n equal to the
-d burden work
the end is nothing
-s inside the slain
-n thud of spears hurled not
on . . . wild asses . . . are
words no longer
nothing is known

JULIANUS, PREFECT OF EGYPT, SEPULCHRAL EPIGRAM FOR ARCHILOCHUS

This grave by the sea belongs to Archilochus, who first
  bittered the Muse, tempering her in snake venom,
tame Helicon stained with blood. Ask this man, Lycambes,
  shedding tears for three daughters hanging from nooses.
Pass quietly by, traveler, so that your step doesn't wake
  these wasps sleeping on the poet's tomb.

Theognis

A man can memorize the books of morality and still be vicious, even as he teaches the precepts to others; an illiterate man can be a paragon of moral virtue without ever opening a book. Most fall somewhere in between. Most play both roles unwittingly: lecherous pedant, holy fool. In the ancient *testimonia* Theognis is known as an elegist of "maxims totaling about 2,800 verses, a collection of elegiac addresses to Cyrnus his beloved, and other hortatory precepts." But among these verses encouraging others in the patrician ethics of the aristocracy, there are other lines—of love, of lust, of envy, of emotion that has lost the bit and rides more wildly through the streets—"on which the virtuous life turns its back." Theognis's themes are human excellence and vice, but underneath the arid sterilities of moral axioms is a life whose complexities question the human worth of such rigid morals, and those doubts are found in the verses, too.

What we know of the life veers away from fact. Some say he was from Sicily, others from Attic Megara. His renown flourished in the 59th Olympiad, 544–541 BCE. The poems hint at a calamity—the loss of his fortune—and are filled with the humble pathos of a man trying to live according to a set of values in which he can no longer feel full faith. The young man he loved, Cyrnus, seems to turn away as the other graces turned away: wealth, social standing, vigor of youth. The wisdom years and suffering supposedly bring do little to loosen nostalgia's rueful grasp on mind and heart. The poems bear within themselves that unbroachable chasm between what life should be and what it is, a dissonance which speaks humble and true across the centuries, and makes Theognis, like us, most human. We hear him keep speaking even as the mask falls off.

Muses and Graces, you pupils of your father's eyes,
You came to the wedding of Cadmus singing words
Fair enough, "What's beautiful is loved, what's not isn't."
These words wandered out your deathless mouths.

Not even searching widely across all men
    Would you find any with the sense of one ear—
A single boat could carry them all: men
    Whose tongues and eyes understand shame, men
Whose dirty lucre doesn't haul after it disgrace.

It's idiotic: doing kind things for craven people—
    Like sowing seed in the gray salt sea—
You don't reap on open water any tall crop—
    You do good, and get not a grain,
Even of salt, in return.

No one, Cyrnus, bewildered by ruin or rich by gain
  Is his own cause—the gods are those givers of both.
No one in his heart knows if the work he slaves over
  Ends up good or if pain is what comes to be.
Expecting to be given good often evil comes,
  And thinking evil on its way often good arrives.
No man has what he wants most walk up beside him
  And say hello—his own hard-to-bear helplessness
Holds him back. Men think they think, but nothing is known.
  Only the gods know what's hidden in their minds.

Worst of all is when poverty breaks a good man,
    Worse than gray old-age, Cyrnus, worse
Than cough and tremor. Better to escape, throw
    Yourself off the cliffs to the monsters
In the wild sea, Cyrnus, into those haunted depths.
    When poverty makes a man her bride, bridles him,
What can be said is sacrificed, hooves step on tongues.

I have given you feathers to lift you lightly up
    And fly across the infinite open waters
And all the earth, present at every feast
    And holy meal, perched on many lips,
And young men on clear-voiced pipes will sing
    Your cosmic eros beautiful and loud.
And when you step down in the dark earth,
    Deep into Hell's full-of-wailing home,
Not even death loosens you from your fame,
    But you will be care undecaying for men
Always carrying your name, Cyrnus, across
    The Greek lands endlessly wandering,
Already on islands, where fish pierce the open
    Sea unharvested; not riding horseback,
The shining gifts of the violet-crowned Muses
    Will bear you. For all who love and hurry
After song, you will be what you are, just
    Like the earth, just like the sun.
But when by chance we meet, you've scant regard;
    Like I'm a small child, you cheat me.

But Zeus, fulfill for me, Olympian, my timely prayer—
Give me, against my evils, some good to suffer—
Or let me die, if from my pains no calm can be
Found. For my sorrows let me give sorrows;
That would be luck. But no revenge appears to me
Against the men who stole into my bedroom
And took by force my treasures. I'm a dog
That walked straight through the mountain
Stream's winter flood—I shake everything off.

He’s a child who keeps watch on what my mind holds
    And doesn’t turn around to guard his own.

. . . those who do not die give
Sudden gifts of many kinds to those who do. Submit,
You must. Wed yourself to the gifts the gods give,
Whatever those gifts are.

Never hold a man back against his will
    to remain among us; never kick him out
the door to the streets when he doesn't want
    to go; never rouse from rest, Simonides,
any of us who, drunk on wine, gentle sleep
    embraces; never send a wakeful man
to bed when he doesn't want to go.
    All force kills joy. For the man wanting
to drink, let the pourer of wine stand beside him.
    But not every night can be so delicate.
And I've drunk all I can drink of honey-sweet wine,
    and going home I'll remember
the pains sleep loosens, undresses, puts to bed.

Your journey, Clearistus, across the deep sea ends here
    broke—o money on the scale—one pan holding nothing.
But I'll give you the best of what I have. And if some dear
    friend of yours drops by, let friendship lean you back.
I won't hide away anything I have, but I won't mingle
    with strangers to carry home gifts from other places.
Under the benches, next to the ribs of your boat, Clearistus,
    I'll stow what I have and give what the gods give.
And if anyone asks about my life, tell them this:
    "To those whose life is good his is grievous, for those
whose life is grievous his is good, kind port to a friend
    of the family, but others are strange ships that sail by."

That "this thing will never be," you must not
make your oath. The gods get wrathful
rightly, and what happens belongs to them.
What's more, what doesn't occur is theirs.
And from evil, good is born; from good, evil.
And also the poor man so quickly
becomes rich, and the man who has gained
much wealth in a single night is suddenly
destroyed; sane minds fall apart; fame often
speaks glory to fools; and a bad man
puts on his ill-gotten cloak of honor.

It's the same for the rich, with all their silver coins
    and gold and flat land bearing wheat
and horses and mules, and all needed by the hearth,
    pot-bellied, fat on the ribs, beer and wine to guzzle
down, all that life likes and likes life, a child and wife
    when the season arrives, a harmony coming
to be in his youthful prime. These are riches
    for those who die—for no one carries all
his countless coins with him as he walks into death,
    no ransom releases you: sickness's slow
weight gathers; old age suddenly stands up inside you.

If you should place a bet, Academus, on singing desire's song,
    the prize a boy holding youth's lovely bloom,
and your skill competed with mine, you would know
    how much mightier mules are than asses.
Then the sun in the sky his hoofed horses urges on
    now to noon's high point holding,
we might be finishing lunch, our hearts urging us on
    to the various good morsels our stomachs crave,
and quick carrying the water basin outside, the Spartan girl
    returns, with laurel crowns in her slender hands.

SEPULCHRAL LINES BY THE AUTHOR HIMSELF

I don't lust after a royal couch to sleep on
  when I'm dead, just that some good thing
may come to me living. A thick carpet
  of thorns spread out as bedsheets is fine
for the dead; for that strange guest, the bitterly
  hard is as soft as the soft-plowed field.

Alcman

A singer has many mothers; the root grows more complicated the deeper it goes.

Two mothers claim Alcman: Sardis in Lydia; Sparta in Laconia. Considered famous by the 30th Olympiad, Alcman must have been born around the 680s BCE. He grew up the household slave of a man named Agesidas, who set him free for his talent. So it proves true, what Emerson said, that the poet is "a liberating god." If he had stayed in his homeland (so imagines Alexander of Aetolia) he "would have been an acolyte carrying the offering-dish or a eunuch-priest wearing gold ornaments, striking the noisy tambourine." He became, instead of a castrated holy-man, a singer of love and lust—the first poet to write amatory poems. His songs he learned listening to the nightingales sing by the waters of the Eurotas; partridges, he says, taught him his poems.

In Sparta he led choruses of daughters and sons, crafting maiden-songs for virgin voices. For the beauty of his craft some say Sparta made him a citizen; some say no. He was the author of six books of lyric poetry and *The Divining Women*, none of which remain. Like the nightingales who tutored him in his art, we hear only the tattered echoes of the songs as they fade deeper into the woods—that forest called *time*.

It is said Homer died from being confounded by the riddle of some fisher-boys. The blind poet asked them of their luck on the waves. They replied, "What we have caught we left behind; what we missed we bring home with us." Bewildered, he wandered the shore, wasting away in confusion, according to some sources, according to others, tripping and knocking his head on a rock.

Alcman died, according to Aristotle, of too much moisture in the body. The symptom of his ailment: a small lesion without pus from which, if pricked, lice would emerge.

It seems a lesson, though I don't know what to learn from it. The epic poet dies from seeking an answer to a riddle, and the answer is the word "lice." Not the riddle and not the word, the love poet dies from the bodily, mortal fact. Lice kill the love poet, too.

Muses, fill up my heart like—
like wine fills a cup with desire
for a new song. I'm eager to hear
virgin voices in lyric air
sing praise to beautiful heaven.
. . . they
scatter sweet sleep on my eyes,
. . . guiding me among
the gathered singers, I will swiftly
shake my yellow hair grown
long as reed-grass. . .
. . . soft feet

. . . and with limb-loosening desire, more
than sleep does or does death, her look melts me—
and that sweetness is no vain thing.

But Astymeloisa doesn't answer me—
doesn't bring me plaited wreaths
or any radiant as heaven
unfolding star
or golden apple or softly stripped bare . . .

. . . long-flowing she passed through—
a Cyprian oil's charm sets down and dampens
the girl's loose-flowing hair . . .

Astymeloisa steps among the mob
the city's darling . . .
                . . . grasping
                . . . I say
        . . . a silver cup

   . . . were she somehow to love me,
came nearer, grasped my soft hand,
how sudden I'd be her suppliant.

Now . . .   girl mind-deep . . .

girl . . .   me holding . . .
                    . . . the girl
                      . . . grace

It's not Aphrodite, but Eros like a feral child,
    playing as a child plays,
stepping down among the flower heads—do not,
    for my sake, take hold of them—the galingale.

These words and the music they ride Alcman
discovered by putting together
the tuneful tongued cackle of partridges

*

And of the birds I know all
the laws and customs

She gave birth to three seasons, summer
and winter, autumn third,
and fourth the spring, when
sprouts grow, and there's nothing to eat.

Often on the mountaintops, when
the festival's many torches please the many gods,
you hold a golden bowl, a great cup
as shepherds also hold,
with your hands pour in a lioness's milk,
and for the slayer of Argus, make cheese with a thick rind.

They are sleeping, mountain-heads, headlands,
and the gullies, too—
the fallen leaves and the tribe of slow-footed
creatures the dark earth grows—
beasts of prey mountain-bred and brood
of wild bees and the brute
monsters deep in the deep purple seas:
and that flock of omen-giving birds long-winged,
they are sleeping, too.

. . . will overhear

. . . sea-toss perplexity of children also

. . . songs cannot be caught

. . . the good work hard

ON TANTALUS

Among pleasing things he sat, the sinner,
under a rock, seeing nothing, imagining all.

necessity is a narrow, pitiless path

*

the mind maimed blind begins the lesson

*

a kind of
        ear-ring

SEPULCHRAL POEM FOR ALCMAN, BY ANTIPATER OF THESSALONICA

Don't judge the man by the rock that ends him—
    the tomb is simple to look at, but it holds
the bright bones of a great man. Do you see him,
    does your mind remember? Alcman: eminent
striker of the Spartan lyre, one of the nine
    poets eternal, number of the Muses. Here he rests—
giver of strife to two lands, Lydia and Sparta, both
    claim him their own. Makers of song have many mothers.

Callimachus

[Epigrams]

Callimachus lived some 350 years after Alcman, the most ancient of the poets translated here, a span of time comparable to the distances separating a contemporary poet to Milton or to Shakespeare. He could still hear Homer in the air, but felt that age of the epic—with its formulated phrases and rituals, its stock catalogs and endless similes—had passed anciently away, and sought instead to write poems that glittered with the sophistications of Ptolemaic Alexandria, where he worked, wrote, and lived. Those hopes led to the writing of more than eight hundred books in every metrical form of poetry, as well as books in prose. The poetic fertility of that Egyptian city during Ptolemy's reign has few parallels in the history of the world's great cities of learning, and Callimachus—trained as a grammarian—had more access to those wonders than most. Though disputed in some sources as to what position he actually held, it is generally accepted that Callimachus became head librarian of the Great Library (which housed some five hundred thousand volumes) after Zenodotus died (260 BCE).

Before his time in the Great Library, Callimachus was a teacher in Eleusis and Alexandria. One of his students, Apollonius of Rhodes, became an equally famous poet. His *Argonautica* prized most the very poetic values Callimachus questioned, and sought to revivify and honor the Homeric age. The literary feud that followed reverberates even now in those ongoing debates between the "major" poem and the "minor"—between the want to write a poem that "justifies the ways of God to man" or, more humbly, to write "some philosophic song / of Truth that cherishes our daily life." Callimachus chose the day.

Of the extant work—the *Aetia*, the *Hymns*, one thousand lines on Theseus and the Bull of Marathon, various occasional poems—I've translated from his collection of *Epigrams*, poems modeled on those sepulchral poems found in *The Greek Anthology*. Those poems, homages and exercises that often alter into their own humble greatness, keep alive the ancient slippage within the Greek words *mnema* and *sema*—those words meaning at one and the same time *memory* and *word* and *memorial*, *sign* and *grave*. So it is the poem knows the grave speaks for itself, and when the poem says "I" it speaks not exactly of a personality buried in the ground, but the ground itself is "I": location of a curiously ongoing life, though the life no longer is living and doesn't speak exactly for itself. The grave speaks it: the singing tomb that is a poem.

II

Someone mentioned, Heracleitus, your death, and brought me
to tears, reminding me how many times together
we put the sun down in his couch to sleep. But somehow you,
Halicarnassian friend, long, long ago, turned to ash.
Your nightingales still live—and that thief Hades, who steals
everything,
will not take those birds in his hands and throw them down.

IV

Don't smile seeing me, with your whole cruel heart, but step
    past—
  to be happy for me is for you to not laugh.

VIII

He wreathed into a crown twigs stripped off a tree,
for a small stone, the grave of his stepmother,
supposing her life altered changed her nature, too.
But her tomb leaned over and, falling down,
sent the boy away to death. All you children firstborn,
run away from the grave rites of stepmothers.

X

Can Charidas be found underneath you? “If you mean
    the son of Arimma of Cyrene, under me.”
Charidas, what of what's below? “Much darkness.”
    What of what's above? “A lie.” And Pluto?
“A tale for a child.” Then we are destroyed.
    “My word is your truth. But if pleasant words
please you, a small coin buys a great ox in hell.”

XIX

If swift ships never were how good it would be—
then we wouldn't be groaning for Sopolis,
son of Diocleides. Now he is carried somewhere
by the sea his corpse belongs to, and we have
a name on an empty grave none see as they pass by.

XXVI

I am my own image, a hero, put by Eetion
    of Amphipolis by his door—small
statue on a small porch, holding only a sword,
    a snake coiling my foot. And that man
Epeius, I'm angry at, too—making me
    a foot-soldier at the corner of his house.

XXVIII

I lived a small life of few hopes, of doing
no awful deed, of being unjust to no one.
Earth I love, if I praised anything wretched,
never lighten your weight that presses me down;
spirits, never hold up for me your lights.

XXXIII

In the hills the hunters hunt, Epikydes, all
the rabbits, walk all the deer-paths the deer
walk, the snow on loan from the sky.
And was anyone to say, "There! There is
the wild beast brought down," he wouldn't take it.
So is my love: pursuing what flees,
leaving behind what lies waiting and wounded.

XXXIX

These gifts for Aphrodite
Simon the wanderer, as last resort, gave—
her living image, the girdle
that bound lovingly her breasts, this torch,
and the ivy-wound wand, poor girl, she always carried.

XLIII

If willfully, Archinus, I serenaded you, then multiply
  my guilt ten thousand times; but if I came against my will,
lay off your hasty judgment. Wine and Love
  tortured me until I complied—of them, from them,
I started out, but I didn't howl out, your name or your father's,
  just kissed the doorpost. If this is wrong, then I'm wrong.

XLIV

The stranger had a wound he couldn't see—you knew him
    by his troubled breath. But when he drank
his third cup he knew himself again: those roses
    he wore as a crown shed all their petals on the ground.
Someone scorched him badly. I swear, gods, the image
    I sing dances true: a robber-bee myself,
I know the pollen-trace a thief leaves behind.

LIX

Who are you, shipwrecked stranger? Leontichus found you,
    a corpse right here on the shore, heaped up the sand
for your funeral rites, shed tears that life is death's subject.
    And you don't rest in peace: the sea wilds itself
into worse waves, and you keep trying to walk across it.

ACKNOWLEDGMENTS

I'm thankful to the editors who published some of these poems in their journals: *AzonaL*, the *Carolina Quarterly*, the *Cincinnati Review*, *Harvard Review*, and the *New England Review*.

Many thanks to Isak Applin of Titan and Weald press, for creating a beautiful broadside of the Simonides poem, titled here, "Of a Castrated Worshipper of Cybele."

Many thanks to Martin Corless-Smith, who published a suite of these poems in his generous chapbook series, *Free Poetry*.

I gladly bear a sense of continual gratitude for Milkweed Editions—this press has made itself a home for me, and I know there is no better gift. Thank you to Daniel Slager, whose vision Seedbank is, and for inviting me to be part of this true, good work. & thank you to the whole team, whose care and vision are sustaining: Yanna Demkiewicz, Mary Austin Speaker, Lee Oglesby, Shannon Blackmer, Claire Laine, and Joey McGarvey.

& lastly, thank you to the friends who read these poems and encouraged me on this inspiring, difficult path of translation: Srikanth Reddy, Sally Keith, Martin Corless-Smith, Kristen Case, Kylan Rice, Sasha Steensen, Aby Kaupang, Matthew Cooperman, and Kristen Case. Thank you to Ian Oliver, who helped me begin studying the language. Thank you to the Monfort family, and my colleagues at CSU—especially Louann Reid, Ann Gill, and Ben Withers—for the gift of the Monfort Professorship, which allowed me the time to begin this work.

This small book of old songs is dedicated to Kristy, whose face is *quicker than sparrows*.

Kristy Beachy-Quick

DAN BEACHY-QUICK is a poet, essayist, and translator. His work has been supported by the Lannan, Monfort, and Guggenheim Foundations. He is a University Distinguished Teaching Scholar at Colorado State University, where he teaches in the MFA Program in Creative Writing.

ABOUT SEEDBANK

Just as repositories around the world gather seeds in an effort to ensure biodiversity in the future, Seedbank gathers works of literature from around the world that foster reflection on the relationship of human beings with place and the natural world.

SEEDBANK FOUNDERS

The generous support of the following visionary investors makes this series possible:

Anonymous
Meg Anderson and David Washburn
The Hlavka Family

Founded as a nonprofit organization in 1980,
Milkweed Editions is an independent publisher. Our mission
is to identify, nurture and publish transformative literature,
and build an engaged community around it.

milkweed.org